RAZZ DAZZLE

David Bateson

Illustrated by Marjory Gardner

Momentum
Razzle Dazzle

First published in Great Britain in 1999 by

Folens Publishers
Albert House
Apex Business Centre
Boscombe Road
Dunstable
Beds LU5 4RL

© 1999 Momentum developed by Barrie Publishing Pty Limited
Suite 513, 89 High St, Kew, Vic 3101, Australia

David Bateson hereby asserts his moral right to be identified as the author of this work in accordance with the Copyright, Designs and Patents Act 1988.
© 1999 Folens Ltd. on behalf of the author.
Illustrations copyright Marjory Gardner.

All rights reserved. No part of this publication may be reproduced or transmitted in any form or by any means, electronic or mechanical, including photocopying, recording or any information storage and retrieval system, without written permission from the publisher.

British Library Cataloguing in Publication Data.
A Catalogue record for this book is available from the British Library

ISBN 1 86202 728 5

Designed by Tom Kurema
Printed in Singapore by PH Productions Pte Ltd

Contents

    5

    9

    15

    19

    25

Chapter One

Twins Wanted

There was one thing my twin sister Vicky and I both hated. It was hanging around outside the laundrette on Saturday morning, waiting for Aunt Lulu.

"Boring," said Vicky.

"Boring," I moaned.

"Listen, Ricky," said Aunt Lulu, giving me her toughest look. "I do the laundry. All I ask you two to do is carry the bags back to the flat."

To make matters worse, today was the start of the vacation. The waiting seemed longer than ever.

I tapped the laundrette window. "Just take a look at these ads."

We weren't interested in the usual ones like FLAT FOR RENT and MICROWAVE FOR SALE. Suddenly, Vicky grabbed my arm. "Take a look at this one. At last, Ricky, here's our big chance to get into show business!"

I stared at the notice.

"Razzle!" I said.
"Dazzle!" said Vicky.

At that moment Aunt Lulu, in her snappy red tracksuit, came marching out of the laundrette. "What's all the hoo-hah about?"

We both pointed at the ad.

"Ah, the theatre," she murmured. "Remember how I told you about spending my younger days in showbiz?"

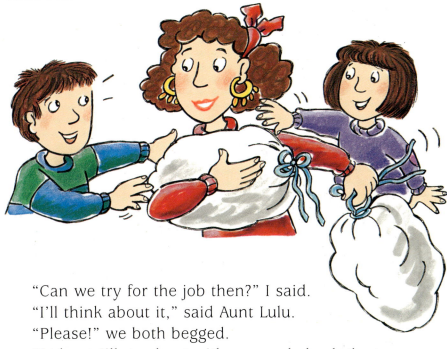

"Can we try for the job then?" I said.

"I'll think about it," said Aunt Lulu.

"Please!" we both begged.

"At least I'll go along with you and check the place out."

"Whammy!" I yelled.

"Double whammy!" yelled Vicky.

"First," warned Aunt Lulu, "you must take the laundry bags home."

We carried them home twice as fast as usual.

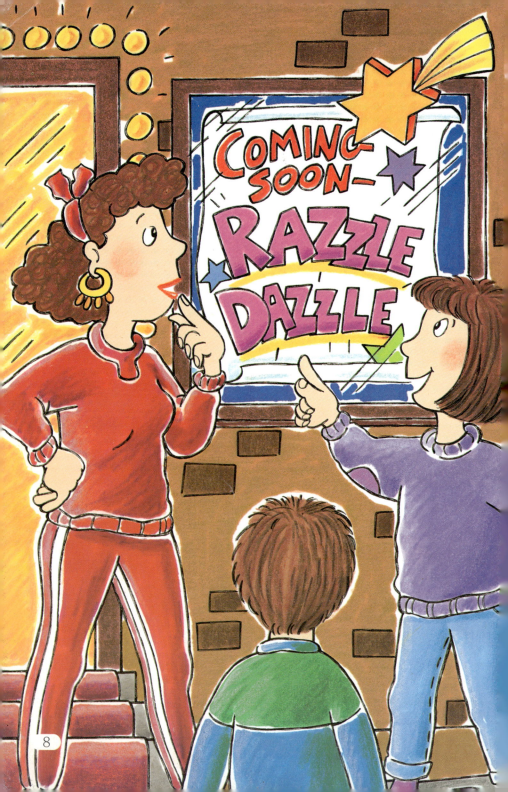

Chapter Two

Mister Misto

As soon as we dumped the laundry in the flat, we hustled off to the theatre, almost at jogging speed. Near the entrance to the theatre there was a Razzle Dazzle poster. One glimpse of this was enough to make Aunt Lulu join in our enthusiasm.

"Many years ago," she explained, "I appeared in a show at this very same theatre."

"I bet you were a star," said Vicky.

"No, I was a chorus girl." She smiled. "Tip Top Tappers, they called us."

There was an alleyway at the side of the theatre. A man was standing outside the stage door. He was shaking with fury.

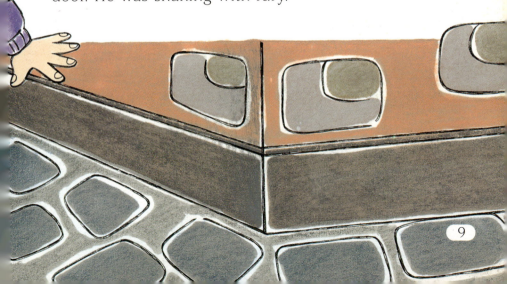

"Take a look at that man," I said. "Black cloak, black top hat, black moustache, black sideburns. That just has to be Mister Misto."

He was scowling at two other children. "You kids can't fool the Magic Man," he roared. "You look as much like twins as Snow White and Tom Thumb."

"We don't look alike right now," whispered Vicky. "I'm in short jeans and Ricky is in long shorts."

"Don't be silly," said Aunt Lulu. "If Ricky was wearing Grandad's nightshirt and you were in the cat's pyjamas, you'd still look alike."

She put her arms around our shoulders and marched us up to the stage door.

"Meet Ricky and Vicky," she announced in her grand manner. "These are genuine twins."

The Magic Man peered at us like a judge in a pet show. "They don't look very much alike. The boy's hair is shorter."

"He could wear a wig," suggested Vicky.

"Or you could have your hair cut off!" I said, glaring at her.

"However," said Misto, "if I decide to put them in my show, the costumes will fix that problem."

"What will we have to do?" I asked.

"Can you walk on a tightrope?" said Misto.

We shuffled our feet and shook our heads.

"Can you do a backward somersault on a flying trapeze?"

We shook our heads again.

"Can you juggle three soup plates and three ping-pong balls at the same time?"

"No, but I can catch a Frisbee on my head," I said.

Misto didn't appear impressed. "What about gymnastics?"

We smiled, nodding frantically.

"Follow me," he ordered. Misto jerked a thumb towards the stage. "Show me what you can do."

We hesitated.

"Try cartwheels and handstands for starters," prompted Aunt Lulu.

Vicky did six cartwheels and a somersault. I stood on my head, then walked on my hands.

Misto said, "At least you don't look like a pair of wooden puppets. But you must both learn to do the gymnastics exactly like each other."

After Aunt Lulu wrote our permission note, we promised to be back at the theatre in an hour, and off we went.

"Razzle!" I said.

"Dazzle!" said Vicky.

"Razzle Dazzle!" we both said.

Chapter Three

The Giant Saw

"Put these costumes on," Misto ordered when we arrived back at the theatre. "Down the steps, first dressing room on the left."

The costumes he handed to us were red-and-yellow jester suits. The head coverings hid our hair. We really looked like each other now.

On stage, Misto snapped at us.

"Pay attention. This act will be a brand-new version of sawing a lady in half. This time I will saw a jester in half!"

"Goodbye, Mister Misto!" I said. "I must get busy with my dinosaur project."

"And I need to clean my skate blades," said Vicky.

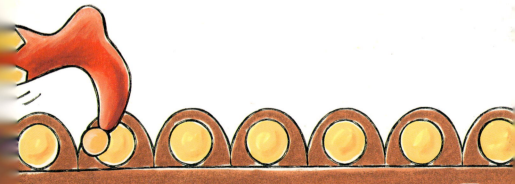

"Not so fast," ordered Misto. "This trick may sound a bit scary, but it's as safe as houses."

"How safe are houses?" murmured Vicky. "How about houses that get wrecked in storms?"

"No need to worry, once you know how it is done," Misto assured us. "But this trick is top secret. You must tell nobody. Promise?"

"Cross my heart and hope to die," said Vicky.

"Cross my heart and hope to live," I said.

"Pepso!" shouted Misto, clapping his hands.

A clown appeared. Pepso had short, thick legs, ears like lollipops, and a nose like a bent carrot.

"Bring in the Box of Destiny," ordered Misto.

Pepso wheeled a trolley in from the wings. On top was a long box, painted purple. There was a hole at one end, big enough for somebody to get inside. A hole at the other end was for feet to stick out. On top of the box there was a huge saw. The teeth looked as fearsome as a tiger's. Vicky's eyes looked like they were ready to pop out. I felt my toes beginning to tingle.

"Calm down, you two," said Misto. "I'm not going to polish you off. After all, I will need you for the next performance."

For the next few days we had rehearsals for hours on end. We had to get the timing perfect. Aunt Lulu was busy in the daytime, but she kept asking about the act when she got home. We told her we didn't want to spoil the surprise. At last, the day came for the opening of the show!

Chapter Four

Showtime

For the big performance, we had to be at the theatre an hour before the show started. Aunt Lulu would come along later, so she ordered a cab for us.

"In the meantime," she announced, "I'll be putting on my glad rags and warpaint."

When we arrived at the theatre, there was already a buzz of excitement. Flashing lights glittered on a huge Razzle Dazzle sign. Backstage, the tension was beginning to build up. There were so many star performers bustling around the place, I began to feel less important. Musicians were busy checking their trumpets and trombones. Dancers were putting on gaudy costumes and tap shoes. There were trapeze artists, jugglers, a fire-eater, a sword swallower and a stand-up comic.

Vicky let Misto see that we had arrived promptly. I sneaked behind the scenes to check out the trolley and box. In my mind I kept going over my part of the magic act in Misto's Box of Destiny.

"Get moving, kid," Pepso shouted at me. "You should be in that jester outfit by now."

"House lights!" came a voice over the intercom.

In the orchestra pit, the band began to play 'It's Magic'. It was time to raise the curtain! Out came the dancers, tapping to a new tune called 'Razzle Dazzle Rock'.

I could imagine Aunt Lulu enjoying all the acts from her seat in the front row. The audience laughed as a stand-up comic did his patter. They clapped as the trapeze artists did their stuff.

In the dressing room, we were waiting in our jester costumes. Suddenly, Pepso the clown poked his head around the door. "Come on, Ricky," he snapped, "time for you to crawl into your box."

"He must be the world's most serious clown," I murmured.

Without another word, I followed him up the steps. We tiptoed past the jugglers waiting to go on, then behind Misto's trolley. There were secret panels in the box. I had to hide in the space behind one of them.

Pepso lifted a lid on top. "In you go."

He hoisted me up, then I had to lower myself into the compartment. It was a tight squeeze, and very dark, even with the airholes.

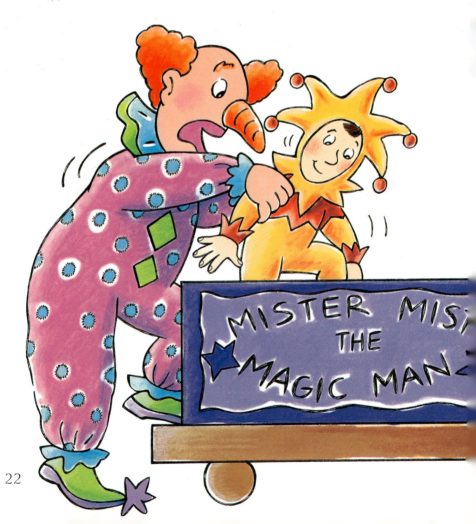

On stage, the jugglers finished amid a flurry of music and a burst of applause. A minute later, there was a trumpet fanfare, the roll of drums and the magic act began. I could tell that Misto was performing a trick I'd seen him do with giant playing cards. It was called 'Find the Queen of Hearts'. After that came the sound of Pepso bringing out a tray of drinks. The audience laughed. I could even hear Aunt Lulu. Misto had to make the drinks vanish in a puff of smoke. The trick must have worked well, for the laughter gave way to applause.

There was another fanfare. My turn was coming at last. Would I be able to get the timing right and help Vicky to make the trick work?

Chapter Five

Mad Magic

"Now, Pepso," commanded Misto, "bring in the giant saw and the Box of Destiny."

I felt the trolley below me vibrate as Pepso wheeled it onto the stage.

"Ladies and gentlemen," said Misto, "you may see for yourselves that there is nothing but air inside this box."

Misto raised a flap at the front. To the audience, it seemed that the box was empty. Then came a really clever part. As Misto let the flap drop down I touched a hidden switch. The secret panels swung forward into the middle of the box. I moved into a squatting position with my feet near to the opening at the end. This made me feel a bit less cramped. Better still, a tiny airhole let me peek through at the audience.

"Ladies and gentlemen," announced Misto, "let me introduce Razzle the Jester."

That was Vicky's cue to do cartwheels onto the stage. The audience must have liked this. They applauded her performance.

"Now, Razzle, you can have a nice little rest," said Misto. "Climb inside my Box of Destiny."

Vicky climbed in, feet first. A tap on the box was the signal to me. Out popped my feet at the other end. Everything was okay so far.

"I wonder what will happen," called Misto to the audience, "if I use the giant saw to cut right through the middle of the box."

There was silence for a moment, then a girl called out, "The jester will get hurt."

"There'll be two halves," a boy shouted. "Blood everywhere."

"It's only a trick," said another boy. "The jester will come back to life in one piece."

Through the airhole, I caught a glimpse of Aunt Lulu, wearing her purple dress with gold trimmings. No doubt she had seen the 'sawing the lady in half' trick before. But her hand moved to cover her mouth and her eyes were closed.

There came an awesome rolling of the drums. Misto moved behind the trolley and began to use the giant saw. Backwards and forwards went the saw, to the sound of a steady drumbeat. I knew it wasn't cutting through the thick wood. It was simply moving down a hidden slot between the panels. But the audience couldn't tell. Down and down went the saw, until it stopped at the trolley.

"Now what have I done?" Misto asked the audience solemnly.

"Let's find out," shouted Pepso.

Misto began to pull gently on Vicky's head, and the clown began tugging my feet. Some people gasped. Some laughed nervously. One person stifled a scream.

There came a crash of cymbals. Suddenly, as fast as I could, I wriggled so that Pepso could pull me out through the end of the box. Vicky emerged just as fast at the other end. Arms raised, we danced to the front of the trolley. There was a thunderous boom on the big drum, a fanfare of trumpets, then a stunned silence from the audience.

"When I saw a jester in two," announced Misto, "what do I get? Two jesters!"

    Some people clapped and others laughed as we did identical cartwheels around the stage. In our costumes, we must have looked exactly alike.

    "Ladies and gentlemen," announced Misto, "meet Razzle and Dazzle!"

People began clapping as he took us by the hand, leading us forward for a bow. Some of the audience, including Aunt Lulu, still looked stunned.
"It's only a trick," said a boy in the third row.
"Yeah, but how does he do it?" gasped another.

It was time for a final number by the dancers, and then the show was over. Along with an excited Aunt Lulu, we were invited to Misto's party on the stage.

Vicky anxiously asked Aunt Lulu, "We can be in the next show, can't we?"

Aunt Lulu smiled. "If Mister Misto can put up with the pair of you."

"With a new trick, maybe?" I suggested.

Misto's eyes glinted. "Would you like to be in my Nervous Knife Thrower act?"

I gulped. "Maybe I'd better stick to being a jester."